First Journeys

By Pamela Rushby

CELEBRATION PRESS
Pearson Learning Group

The following people from **Pearson Learning Group**
have contributed to the development of this product:

Joan Mazzeo, Dorothea Fox **Design** | **Editorial** Leslie Feierstone-Barna, Cindy Kane
Christine Fleming **Marketing** | **Publishing Operations** Jennifer Van Der Heide
Production Laura Benford-Sullivan
Content Area Consultant Dr. Daniel J. Gelo

The following people from **DK** have
contributed to the development of this product:

Art Director Rachael Foster

Martin Wilson **Managing Art Editor** | **Managing Editor** Marie Greenwood
Janice English **Design** | **Editorial** Marian Broderick
Brenda Clynch **Picture Research** | **Production** Gordana Simakovic
Richard Czapnik, Andy Smith **Cover Design** | **DTP** David McDonald
Consultant Philip Wilkinson

Dorling Kindersley would like to thank: Fred English for orginal illustration. Simon Mumford for cartography. Polly Appleton for additional design. Julie Ferris, Penny Smith, and Selina Wood for editorial help. Rose Horridge, Gemma Woodward, and Hayley Smith in the DK Picture Library. Johnny Pau for additional cover design work.

Picture Credits: AKG London: 8tl, 9tl, 12cr2, 18t. The Art Archive: Bibliotheque Nationale Paris 6. B.C. Archives: 15b. Corbis: 22tl, 23br; Bettmann 18bl, 24tl, 24-25; John Madere 11br. Canadian Pacific Railway: 14t, 15t. DK Images: Beaulieu Motor Museum 17b, 18br; National Maritime Museum 7cr; National Railway Museum York/Science Museum 13; Pitt Rivers Museum 4tr. Mary Evans Picture Library: 16; Leadenhall Press 4b. Getty Images: Adam Smith 5b. The Kon-tiki Museum, Oslo, Norway: 11tr. NASA: HSFC 29cr, 29b; JSC 29tr, 31tl, 31tr; KSC 30; MSFC 28l. National Air and Space Museum, Smithsonian Institution: 1tr, 23tr; Smithsonian Institution 22b. National Motor Museum, Birdwood, Australia: 19b. Newspix Archive/Nationwide News: 23cl. Novosti (London): 26b, 27t. Pa Photos: EPA 3, 10tl, 10bl. Reuters: 5t. Science & Society Picture Library: National Railway Museum 12bl. Science Photo Library: 1b, 12cr, 17t; Novosti 27b, 28b. Roger Viollet: 7tr. Special Collections and Archives, Wright State University: 20cr, cr2, 20-21b, 21tr. Jacket: Corbis: Bettmann front t. DK Images: Beaulieu Motor Museum back; National Railway Museum, York front bl.

All other images: Dorling Kindersley © 2005. For further information see www.dkimages.com

ISBN: 0-7652-5268-6

Color reproduction by Colourscan, Singapore
Printed in the United States of America
2 3 4 5 6 7 8 9 10   08 07 06 05

1-800-321-3106
www.pearsonlearning.com

Contents

First Journeys

People begin long journeys every day. They board airplanes or high-speed trains, or jump in a car and turn on the ignition, never questioning how the transportation works. They just settle back and enjoy the ride. However, travel was not always so routine. Until a few hundred years ago, except for soldiers and some craftspeople and traders, many people never moved very far from the place where they were born.

Compasses helped the first Chinese explorers to navigate long journeys.

The first travelers moved from place to place on foot. Later, people rode on horses, camels, and other animals, such as donkeys. About 5,000 years ago, people began using wheeled vehicles to transport themselves and their goods when they traveled. Ancient Egyptians were using sailboats about this time.

Steam power drove the earliest engines.

Traveling by plane is now an everyday event.

Travel did not improve much over the thousands of years that followed. It wasn't until the development of the steam engine in the eighteenth century that travel started to change. Steam locomotives and steamships revolutionized travel on land and at sea. After this point, the history of travel is linked to the invention of increasingly powerful engines.

Throughout history, people have tried to invent better ways to get from place to place. It is human nature to create new things. However, inventors have also been driven by the rewards awaiting those who could make travel quicker, cheaper, and easier. In *First Journeys,* you will read about how and why the way people travel has changed and also find out about some amazing inventions and "firsts" in the world of travel.

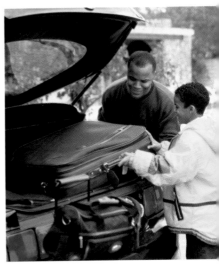

Car ownership makes it easier for people to travel.

Boats and Ships

No one knows who invented the first boat. Some early cultures used boats made of animal skins stretched over wooden frames. Many other early cultures used dugouts, boats made of hollowed-out logs. The first sailing vessels probably originated in Egypt around 3000 B.C. For thousands of years, people traveled by boats and ships over seas, lakes, and rivers. Then, around 500 B.C., the world's first major canal was built in China.

The Grand Canal of China

China's Grand Canal was built to carry goods from the Chang Jiang (or Yangtze River) in the south to cities in the north. The canal was started in 86 B.C. It was extended many times. In A.D. 605, the Sui emperor Yangdi came to the throne of China. He dreamed of building a grand palace in the new capital city of Luoyang. The new palace was to be filled with treasures: rare flowers, exotic animals, and beautiful works of art. The best way to transport those treasures was by water.

Yangdi decided to extend the Grand Canal to unite northern and southern China. A million workers labored to build the canal. In 610, the emperor celebrated the opening of the Grand Canal with a parade of thousands of boats. In a land where rivers flow from west to east, a canal that flowed from north to south had a huge impact on the movement of people and goods.

The Grand Canal, which is more than 1,000 miles long, remains the world's longest canal.

Admiral Zheng He's Voyages

Zheng He (jung huh), a famous Chinese admiral, made seven voyages of exploration between 1405 and 1433. The admiral was born in 1371 to poor Muslim parents in southwest China. He grew up speaking both Arabic and Chinese, which helped him in his later travels.

Admiral Zheng He

As a boy, he was captured by the Chinese army. He received an education and worked as a servant of a prince who later overthrew the emperor. Zheng served the prince well and helped him in wartime. The new emperor, Yongle, gave Zheng a fleet of ships and told him to sail to the countries beyond the horizon.

Over the years, Admiral Zheng sailed with about sixty-two ships to many lands, including present-day Vietnam, Indonesia, Malaysia, India, Somalia, and Sri Lanka. He returned to China with great riches, such as jewels, ivory, exotic animals, and spices.

The Voyages of Admiral Zheng He

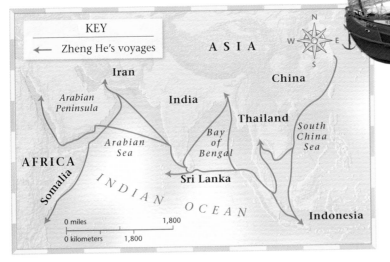

Zheng He's fleet was made up of Chinese sailing vessels called junks. They were the biggest and best ships in the world at the time.

Magellan Journeys West

Ferdinand Magellan

From 1519 to 1522, about a hundred years after Zheng He made his voyages, a European expedition led by Portugal's Ferdinand Magellan became the first to sail completely around the globe.

In 1518, Magellan convinced King Charles I of Spain to pay for a voyage to the Spice Islands. These islands, now called the Moluccas, are part of present-day Indonesia. They were normally reached from Europe by sailing south past the west coast of Africa and then east into the Indian Ocean. Magellan believed the world was round. For this reason, he believed the trip would be shorter if he sailed west and went around the tip of South America. The expedition set out in 1519 with five ships and about 260 men.

However, the voyage had many problems. One of the ships was lost in a storm. The rest of the fleet reached the southern tip of South America in November 1520. Magellan and his ships sailed through a dangerous passage and eventually reached the Pacific Ocean.

The Route of Magellan's *Vittoria*

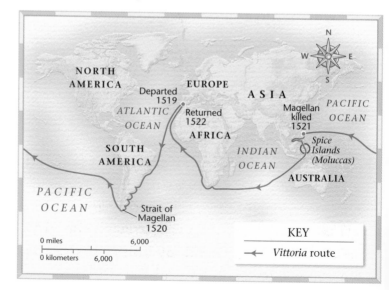

Two ships reached the Spice Islands, but only the *Vittoria* returned to Spain.

As early as 300 B.C., the Spice Islands were visited often by Chinese, Indian, and Arab traders in search of cloves and nutmeg— highly valued spices.

cloves

Magellan, like other explorers of the time, under-estimated the size of the Pacific Ocean. He thought that it would take about three weeks to reach the Spice Islands. Instead, it took about four months. Many of the sailors wanted to return to Spain, but Magellan pressed on. Eventually the food and water ran out. The men had to eat bits of leather and sawdust. Nineteen men died before the fleet arrived in Guam and the sailors were able to restock their food and water. When the ships reached the Philippines, Magellan interfered in a war and was killed in battle.

nutmeg

Just two of Magellan's ships reached the Spice Islands. Only one, the *Vittoria*, returned to Spain, carrying a valuable cargo of spices. The crew of the *Vittoria* had sailed 50,610 miles, and, by doing so, they became the first people to travel around the world.

Heyerdahl Crosses the Oceans

Like Magellan, Norway's Thor Heyerdahl (HI-ur-doll) had theories about sea voyages that were not shared by others of his time. As an anthropologist, Heyerdahl studied ancient peoples and their ways of life. He believed that many ancient civilizations could have had the same roots. He thought perhaps the ancient Peruvians had traveled to islands in the Pacific on primitive boats. Maybe the ancient Egyptians had made similar voyages to the Americas. To test his theories, Heyerdahl made several long and dangerous journeys.

Thor Heyerdahl

In 1947, Heyerdahl successfully sailed a raft called *Kon-Tiki* from Callao, Peru, to the Raroia Atoll on the Tuamotu Archipelago in Polynesia—a distance of 4,300 miles. Heyerdahl covered this distance in 101 days. He'd built his fragile-looking raft with logs from the balsa tree, a light but very strong wood used by the ancient Peruvians. He proved that indigenous South Americans could have migrated to Polynesia in ancient times and could have been the first settlers. Other anthropologists believe that the Polynesians originated in Asia.

The *Kon-Tiki* was built of nine lightweight balsa logs from South America.

In 1969, Heyerdahl attempted to sail a reed boat, the *Ra*, from Safi, in Morocco, North Africa, to Barbados. He hoped to show that ancient Egyptians, who used these simple boats, could have reached the Americas. Just a week from Barbados, the *Ra* broke up and had to be abandoned. Heyerdahl then built a second boat with a different design, based on the reed boats of Lake Titicaca, located between Bolivia and Peru. He sailed this boat, the *Ra II*, in 1970.

Thor Heyerdahl sailed from North Africa to Barbados in the *Ra II*.

This time, his 3,270-mile trip to Barbados was successful, proving that the ancient Egyptians could have reached the Americas.

Thor Heyerdahl's Journeys

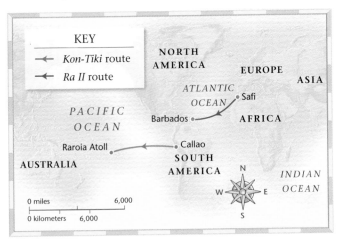

KEY

← *Kon-Tiki* route

← *Ra II* route

NORTH AMERICA
EUROPE
ASIA
ATLANTIC OCEAN
Safi
PACIFIC OCEAN
Barbados
AFRICA
Raroia Atoll
Callao
AUSTRALIA
SOUTH AMERICA
INDIAN OCEAN
N W E S

0 miles 6,000
0 kilometers 6,000

People who live near Lake Titicaca in South America still use boats made of reeds that grow beside the lake.

Train Travel

Most people today would not have wanted to travel on the first railways. The rails were made of wood or iron, and the trains were pulled by horses. The wooden seats were hard, and the ride was usually bumpy. These railways, however, were not meant for passengers. They usually carried coal. The first passenger cars were used in 1825.

The Father of Railways

George Stephenson worked at one of the coal mines in the north of England, running and repairing the mine's steam-driven machinery. A talented engineer, Stephenson decided to design locomotives himself.

George and Robert Stephenson were railway pioneers.

Stephenson built several locomotives for hauling coal. Then, in 1825, he finished his steam engine, the *Locomotion*. On September 27, the engine took its first run of just under 9 miles, with Stephenson at the controls.

The *Locomotion* hauled a load of coal and flour, and a special car for passengers.

For the first time, a train carried people in addition to cargo. Stephenson had designed a special passenger car, which held a group of riders. Cheered on by a crowd, the *Locomotion* reached a top speed of 15 miles per hour.

In 1829, the new Liverpool and Manchester Railway, which would be important in moving not only passengers but also Manchester's textiles to the port at Liverpool, held a competition. The company wanted to choose the best engine for its railway.

Ten engines were entered in the trial, but only five engines arrived on the day of the competition. Two of those had mechanical problems. Three were working well enough to compete. Stephenson's *Rocket* reached a speed of 30 miles per hour and won the prize of £500, worth about $1,800. Stephenson and his son Robert had won by designing an even faster locomotive.

a reproduction of Stephenson's *Rocket* locomotive

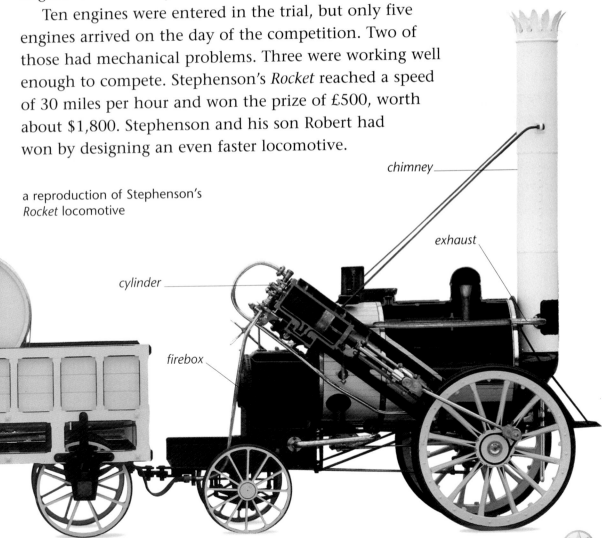

chimney

exhaust

cylinder

firebox

Uniting a Country by Rail

On June 1, 1875, work started on the Canadian Pacific Railway (CPR). It would be the first railroad to cross Canada from coast to coast. Before 1871, the Pacific Coast province of British Columbia was not yet part of Canada. In that year, British Columbia agreed to join the other provinces—but only if the Canadian government promised to build a railway to connect it with the provinces in the east.

The CPR engines followed routes over the Canadian Rockies, passing forests, spectacular lakes, and mountains.

Most of the railway was built between 1881 and 1885. It started in Montréal in the east and ended in Vancouver in the west. The tracks ran along sheer mountain sides, plunging deep into valleys, and crossing wide rivers. A huge amount of dynamite was needed to blast away rocks and cliffs to make way for the railroad. Thousands of Chinese laborers came to Canada to help build the railroad. Many hoped to improve their lives, but often they were given the most dangerous jobs, and many died while working on the railroad. On November 7, 1885, the last spike was driven into the rail in Craigellachie, a town to the east of Vancouver.

Route of the Canadian Pacific Railway

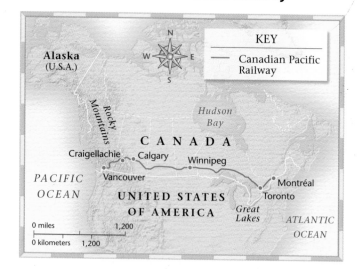

In 1886, the year after the CPR was completed, Canada's first prime minister, Sir John A. Macdonald, decided to cross the country on the railway himself. His wife, Lady Susan Agnes Macdonald, went with him.

Lady Macdonald was an adventurous woman. She thought that while views from the train windows might be spectacular, she'd see more if she was at the front of the train. In fact, she wanted to ride on the cowcatcher! Cowcatchers were designed to push wandering livestock and other obstacles out of the train's way. Seated on a wooden box tied to the front of the train, Lady Macdonald rode on the cowcatcher for part of each day. She enjoyed it so much that she announced, "I shall travel on this cowcatcher from summit to sea!"

railway poster

Many passengers followed Lady Susan Macdonald's example and sat on the cowcatcher.

Early Automobiles

Horse-drawn carriages were still used on roads fifty years after steam-driven passenger trains began running. The trains were faster and far more comfortable than the horse-drawn vehicles, but trains could only go where there was a track. Many places could not be reached by trains.

The first "horseless carriages" were then developed. These self-propelled vehicles were made by the same companies that had built horse-drawn carriages. Inventors of early cars tried many power sources. The most successful early cars ran on steam, although some later cars used electricity. However, these cars were not very practical. The driver of a steam-powered car had to boil water to create the steam to run the car. Drivers of electric cars couldn't go far without recharging the batteries.

The earliest "horseless carriages" were steam-powered. They didn't catch on—perhaps because they moved only as fast as a person can walk!

Karl Benz's Car

Karl Benz

In 1885, a German inventor named Karl Benz designed and built the first automobile powered by gasoline. His first car had three wheels. It also had an electric battery, a spark plug, and a water-cooled engine, just as many cars have today. Benz's car ran at top speeds of more than 5 miles per hour.

Karl Benz planned to take his car for its first drive through the streets of Mannheim, Germany. As he drove toward the open gateway of his workshop yard, he missed the opening and drove straight into a wall. It was the world's first recorded car accident.

Benz kept working on his designs. Soon after 1890, he began selling a four-wheeled car called the Viktoria. It was followed in 1894 by another design called the Velo. So many people were interested in buying the Velo that Benz began thinking of ways to make more cars faster. In 1895, he produced sixty-two Velos— making the car the first automobile produced in larger numbers.

hand brake

water-cooled gas engine

Benz's three-wheeler traveled at about the speed a person can run.

single front wheel

steering wheel

Henry Ford and the Model T

Henry Ford

In 1908, an American engineer named Henry Ford created the first car that really appealed to ordinary people. His Model T car was easy to drive, reasonably priced, and reliable. The public loved it. The Model T became so popular that Ford had to find a new way to produce a huge number of cars.

In the past, cars had been made by groups of two to three workers who built each car from start to finish. Ford began using the same parts, such as fenders, windows, and headlamps, on all the cars. This innovation cut time and costs, and greatly increased production. In 1913, Henry Ford set up assembly lines. Workers stood in one place and performed just one task, such as adding or tightening a part, on every car that moved past them. Another way that Ford streamlined the manufacturing process was by limiting the choice of colors. He said that people could have the Model T in "any color, so long as it's black." When production of Model Ts ended in 1927, 15 million of them had been built.

Model T Ford

Ford's factory eventually cut production time for each car manufactured from days to minutes.

Driving Across Australia

More than 10,000 miles from Henry Ford's assembly lines, two Australians were trying to be the first to drive a "horseless carriage" across Australia from south to north. In late 1907, Harry Dutton and Murray Aunger left Adelaide in a car they had named *Angelina*.

Their route cut across the dry center of Australia, over sandy hills, stony plains, and dry riverbeds. In many places there were no roads— and even today there are very few.

Dutton and Aunger's Route

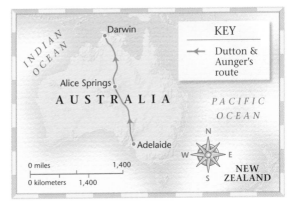

The south-to-north crossing lay over some of the most difficult landscape in Australia.

Before their journey began, camel trains dropped fuel and food at stops along the way. All went well until *Angelina* broke down. Dutton and Aunger didn't give up. They went back to Adelaide and ordered a new, more powerful car. Several months later, the new car arrived from Britain. They set out again—this time, carrying spare parts. They found *Angelina*, repaired it, and then drove both cars side by side on to Darwin. After 51 days, they completed the more than 2,000-mile-long drive on August 20, 1908. In the 1950s, Dutton's sons, Geoff and John, drove *Angelina* along the same route.

Dutton and Aunger crossed Australia from south to north in 1908 in this car.

First Flights

For centuries, humans dreamed of flying. Some built huge flapping wings and tried—unsuccessfully—to fly like birds. Others built gliders, a type of aircraft without engines. Some rode in hot-air balloons that drifted wherever the wind took them. Finally, some people who hoped to fly began to build airplanes.

The Wright Brothers' Flight

Flying fascinated Orville and Wilbur Wright, inventors who lived in Dayton, Ohio, in the United States. Orville and Wilbur made mechanical toys when they were boys. Later, they built and repaired bicycles before designing their plane. The brothers wanted to be the first to build and pilot a powered flying machine. They knew the first thing they needed was a lightweight engine.

Wilbur and Orville Wright

They built a suitable gasoline engine with a propeller, which they believed was powerful enough to thrust, or push, an aircraft forward. Next, they needed to design a plane that would move fast enough so that the air flowing over and under the wings would lift it into the air. The brothers needed to create a design that could overcome the gravity that would naturally pull the plane to Earth and be streamlined enough to slice through the air like a knife, overcoming the drag, or force, that slows down moving objects. Finally, it was time to test their design.

Before he took off, Orville set up the camera to take this photograph. The site of the Wright brothers' flight is now the Wright Brothers National Memorial.

The world's first powered flight, controlled by an onboard pilot, took place at Kitty Hawk, North Carolina. There, Wilbur and Orville tested their plane, the *Flyer*, on December 17, 1903. A few days before, the brothers had tossed a coin to decide who would be the first to fly. When the wind was right, Orville took the controls.

Orville piloted the *Flyer* down a hill, where it wobbled uncertainly into the air. The *Flyer* remained airborne for about 40 yards, then came safely back to Earth. The flight had lasted for just 12 seconds, but it was a historic moment. A human had taken to the sky. It was the first time a pilot had flown a heavier-than-air machine—one that required engine power to stay aloft.

The Wright brothers' propeller design was much more effective than other propellers of the time.

The Father of Aviation

Alberto Santos-Dumont

In his native Brazil, Alberto Santos-Dumont is known as the Father of Aviation. Most of his flying was done in France, where he was studying. Santos-Dumont built and experimented with hot-air balloons and dirigibles, gas-filled airships that can be steered.

In 1901, he won a prize of 100,000 francs (about $17,100) for flying a dirigible around the Eiffel Tower. In 1904, he began to design helicopters and gliders.

By 1906, Santos-Dumont had produced an extra-light flying machine that looked like three kites joined together. On November 12, 1906, Santos-Dumont flew his machine for 240 yards in a 21-second flight. It was the first heavier-than-air flight made in Europe.

Santos-Dumont went on to design a flying machine called an ultra-light monoplane, a plane with only one set of wings. Made of silk stretched over a bamboo frame, it weighed only 150 pounds. The plane was extremely popular, and Santos-Dumont sold thousands of copies. He gave his machine the name *Demoiselle* (duh-mwah-ZEHL), which means "young lady" in French, but others called it the *Grasshopper* because of its insect-like appearance.

Santos-Dumont crashed twice before completing the course that circled the Eiffel Tower.

First, Fastest, and Best

In the early years of aviation, pilots competed to be the best, the first, or the fastest. Charles Lindbergh was the first person to fly solo nonstop across the Atlantic Ocean from New York to Paris. The American pilot took off from Long Island, New York, on May 20, 1927, in a single-engine monoplane, called the *Spirit of St Louis*. Thirty-three hours, 32 minutes, and more than 3,579 miles later, he landed safely in Paris.

Charles Lindbergh's monoplane the *Spirit of St Louis*

Charles Kingsford Smith was an Australian aviator who hoped to be the first person to fly across the Pacific Ocean. His crew of four set off in 1928 from San Francisco, California. Their plane, the *Southern Cross*, had an open cockpit and three engines. The journey of 7,546 miles, with stops in Honolulu and Fiji, took 83 hours. When the plane reached Brisbane, Australia, it was met by 25,000 cheering and excited people.

Charles Kingsford Smith

To earn respect as a pilot, Amy Johnson, of Great Britain, set out to fly from England to Australia in 1930. She faced bad weather, mechanical problems, and crash landings. Johnson had to mend the canvas wings of her plane, *Jason*, along the way. The 9,942-mile journey took her 19 days. Newspapers and radio reporters followed her adventures closely. When she landed in Darwin, Australia, Johnson had become world-famous.

Amy Johnson

Amelia Earhart

Amelia Earhart

In the 1920s, flying was viewed as an activity for men. Very few flying clubs would accept women as members or even as students. Women who wanted to fly had to be very determined indeed.

Amelia Earhart of Kansas was one such woman. She had learned to fly soon after World War I. In 1928, she became the first woman to cross the Atlantic by air. She flew as a passenger, with American pilots Wilmer Stultz and Louis Gordon.

After that, Amelia Earhart became very interested in long-distance flying, and she wanted to fly herself. In 1932, she flew solo across the Atlantic—the first woman to do so. Earhart set a new record for speed. It took her 13 hours and 30 minutes to fly from Newfoundland, Canada, to the British Isles.

Earhart began planning for a new goal. She wanted to fly around the world. After that, she planned to give up long-distance flying. In 1937, Earhart and her navigator, Fred Noonan, flew from California to Florida in a small two-engine plane. Noonan plotted a route from Miami that passed over Puerto Rico, South America, Africa, the Red Sea, India, Thailand, Singapore, and Australia, and landed in New Guinea. They took off on June 1, 1937.

The pair reached Lae, New Guinea, on June 29. They had about 2,500 miles to go until their next stop at Howland Island in the North Pacific Ocean. From there, they planned to return to the United States. The fliers had enough fuel for about 20 or 21 hours of flight.

They lost radio contact somewhere over the ocean, 20 hours 14 minutes after takeoff. Despite an air and sea search that cost more than $4 million, no trace of the plane or its crew was found. In 2002, a marine biologist claimed to have seen a piece of the plane's wreckage on the small island of Nikumaroro. This claim is still being investigated. For now, Earhart's disappearance remains a mystery.

Amelia Earhart's Last Flight

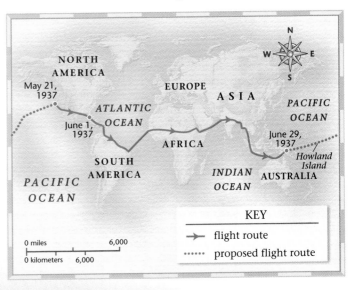

NORTH AMERICA

May 21, 1937

ATLANTIC OCEAN

June 1, 1937

EUROPE

ASIA

PACIFIC OCEAN

AFRICA

June 29, 1937

SOUTH AMERICA

Howland Island

INDIAN OCEAN

AUSTRALIA

PACIFIC OCEAN

N W E S

0 miles 6,000
0 kilometers 6,000

KEY
→ flight route
····· proposed flight route

Fred Noonan and Amelia Earhart looked over their plane before their flight.

Exploring Space

About fifty years after the first airplane flights, people began to look farther and farther out into space. In the 1950s and 1960s, the United States and what was then the Soviet Union, which included Russia, began a race to be the first to travel into space.

Sputnik I carried no living creatures on board.

First Satellites

In 1957, the Soviet Union successfully launched the first artificial satellite, *Sputnik I*. As it orbited, it sent back information about Earth's upper atmosphere. One month later, the Soviet Union launched *Sputnik II*. Scientists wanted to study the effects of space travel on a living animal, so this spacecraft carried a dog named Laika. Three dogs were trained to fly on a spacecraft. The voyage would help scientists prepare to send people into space. Dogs were chosen because their circulatory and respiratory systems are much like those of humans. Laika did not live very long in space, but scientists learned from her experience and were able to improve conditions on the spacecraft. In addition to dogs, rats, mice, monkeys, fish, frogs, bees, and jellyfish have also traveled in space.

Laika in *Sputnik II*

First Human in Space

Yuri Gagarin

After Laika's flight, the Soviet Union sent several unmanned flights into space to gather more data. The Soviet Union then won the first leg of the space race by putting the first human cosmonaut (Soviet astronaut), Yuri Gagarin, into space. On April 12, 1961, he orbited Earth in the Soviet Union's *Vostok 1*.

Gagarin wore a specially designed spacesuit. It had multiple layers, a special breathing valve, a helmet, and communications equipment. He traveled in a capsule only slightly more than 8 feet wide. It took one huge rocket, plus four smaller booster rockets, to launch the capsule into space. The launch rockets were thirteen times bigger than Gagarin's tiny capsule.

After a 108-minute flight that took Gagarin around the world once, he ejected from his craft and parachuted safely to Earth, landing in Siberia, a part of the Soviet Union. Gagarin was a hero to many people.

Vostok 1 carried Gagarin into space.

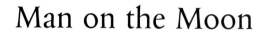

Man on the Moon

About a month after Gagarin's flight, the first American astronaut, Alan Shepard, was launched into space. He made a successful 15-minute flight. Noting the American people's excitement at Shepard's flight, President John F. Kennedy declared that an American would land on the Moon by the end of the 1960s. The space race heated up.

The Soviet Union made some important achievements in the 1960s. Although several Americans had orbited Earth, beginning with John Glenn in 1962, none had spent more than a day in space. Then, in 1963, Soviet cosmonaut Valentina Tereshkova spent nearly three days in orbit. The first woman in space, she circled Earth forty-eight times. However, the Soviet Union's space program suffered a serious blow when the chief designer, Sergei Pavlovich, died in 1966.

The scientists at America's National Aeronautics and Space Administration (NASA) invented ever more sophisticated spacecrafts. American astronauts made space-walking experiments and orbited the Moon, setting the stage for the *Apollo 11* mission.

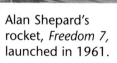

Alan Shepard's rocket, *Freedom 7*, launched in 1961.

Valentina Tereshkova

On July 16, 1969, *Apollo 11* took off from Florida. Its destination was the Moon. On July 20, 1969, millions of people all over the world crowded around televisions and radios as mission commander Neil Armstrong climbed slowly down the ladder of the lunar module *Eagle* and became the first man to set foot on the Moon. His footprints are still visible there today.

Neil Armstrong, Michael Collins, and "Buzz" Aldrin

The other crew members on the mission were Edwin "Buzz" Aldrin, who was second to walk on the Moon, and Michael Collins, who remained in the orbiting command module. On the Moon, Armstrong and Aldrin planted an American flag. They collected rocks and soil samples and set up equipment that would continue to send information back to Earth after they had gone.

Aldrin joined Armstrong on the historic walk. They left footprints where none had been before.

The Space Shuttle

In the next three years, several more American astronauts traveled to the Moon. In six separate *Apollo* flights, astronauts spent 80 hours walking on the Moon, taking photographs, collecting rocks, and setting up experiments. These journeys into space were very expensive. The rocket used to launch a spacecraft could only be used once. Scientists began to consider ways to make spacecrafts reusable.

By the 1980s, a reusable spacecraft became a reality in the United States. The Space Transportation System, or space shuttle, can take astronauts and their equipment into space and then return to Earth to be used again. The shuttle is huge, weighing more than 2,000 tons. The space shuttle has three sections: the orbiter, a fuel tank, and two rocket boosters.

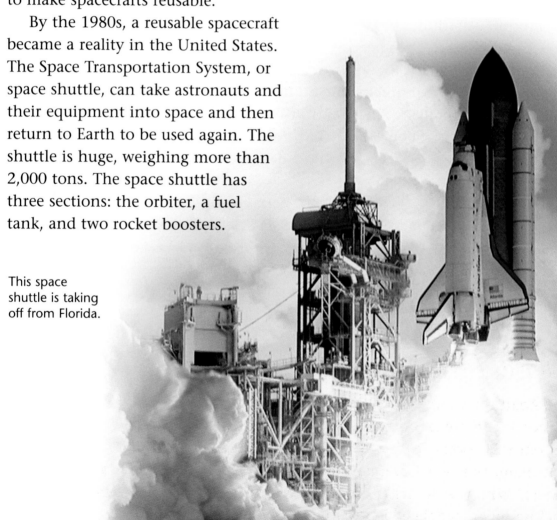

This space shuttle is taking off from Florida.

A space shuttle is seen here with *Mir* space station.

flight deck

payload bay

vertical wing

A space shuttle can orbit Earth many times.

When a space shuttle is launched, the two rocket boosters fall away after liftoff. They are recovered and reused. The fuel tank is designed to fall away and burn up after the shuttle reaches orbit. When the orbiter returns to Earth, it glides in and lands like a plane. The first space shuttle to fly in orbit was launched on April 12, 1981. Since then, there have been many successful space shuttle missions but also some accidents. Scientists are always working to improve the safety and efficiency of the shuttle.

Where to Next?

Apart from our own Earth, the Moon is the only body in space where humans have set foot. Now scientists are looking at our solar system's planets, wondering if humans could live on them. Where will humans journey to next? How will they get there? Who will be first? Like the adventurous men and women before them, people will continue to answer these questions as they journey into the universe's uncharted territory.

Index